The Institute of Biology's
Studies in Biology no. 113

The Nature of
Toadstools

© C. T. Ingold, 1979

First published 1979
by Edward Arnold (Publishers) Limited
41 Bedford Square, London WC1B 3DQ

ISBN: 0 7131 2748 1

British Library Cataloguing in Publication Data

Ingold, Cecil Terence
    The nature of toadstools. – (Institute of Biology. Studies in biology;
    no. 113   ISSN 0537-9024).
    1.   Mushrooms
    I.   Title   II.   Series
    589'.222   QK617

ISBN 0-7131-2748-1

Printed and bound in Great Britain at
The Camelot Press Ltd, Southampton

General Preface to the Series

Because it is no longer possible for one textbook to cover the whole field of biology while remaining sufficiently up to date, the Institute of Biology has sponsored this series so that teachers and students can learn about significant developments. The enthusiastic acceptance of 'Studies in Biology' shows that the books are providing authoritative views of biological topics.

The features of the series include the attention given to methods, the selected list of books for further reading and, wherever possible, suggestions for practical work.

Readers' comments will be welcomed by the Education Officer of the Institute.

1979   Institute of Biology
                                            41 Queen's Gate
                                            London SW7 5BR

Preface

Toadstools (including mushrooms) constitute an important order (Agaricales) of the Kingdom of Fungi. They are of outstanding interest to naturalists and there are few natural history societies that do not hold fungal forays in the autumn. Some toadstools are deadly poisonous but a number are edible. Three have been cultivated for hundreds of years. Many are of great importance in the economy of nature, particularly in the breakdown of organic matter in the soil, and as symbionts in the mycorrhizal association with forest trees assisting their roots in the absorption of inorganic ions. A few, particularly the Honey Fungus, are important parasites, especially of woodland trees. The aim of this booklet is to give an account of the various aspects of toadstool biology: nutrition, genetics, ecology and spore dispersal. The toadstool itself is an apparatus concerned with the production and liberation of millions of spores. Its activity in this respect can readily be studied without the need for any elaborate apparatus, apart from a microscope.

Benson, Oxford, 1978   C. T. I.

Contents

1 Introduction

1.1 The terms 'toadstool' and 'mushroom'

The aim of this booklet is to give an account of certain of the larger fungi, namely mushrooms and toadstools. In no sense is it a guide to their identification. For that, a number of excellent books with the necessary coloured illustrations are available. Rather it aims to describe their nature, to show how they work and to indicate their importance in the economy of nature and to man himself.

Both 'toadstool' and 'mushroom' are English words dating from about the fifteenth century. So far as 'toadstool' is concerned, it seems unlikely that toads are in any way involved. It is more probable that the first syllable comes from the German word 'Tod' (death) and has reference to the evil reputation of the very few deadly poisonous species. Both words are used by naturalists to denote the kind of umbrella-shaped fungus with a circular cap (pileus) and a substantial central stalk (stipe). The popular idea is that toadstools are poisonous, or at least not good to eat, while mushrooms are edible. However, the two words are synonymous in many contexts. Clearly they have no precise scientific meaning. In Britain 'mushroom' is mainly used by mycologists to denote a species of *Agaricus*, but in America the word tends to be applied to any gill-bearing fungus. In this booklet 'toadstool' is employed for any fleshy fungus having a central stipe bearing a discoid cap with gills or pores below (Fig. 1–1). The term 'agaric' is often used by mycologists for any gill-bearing fungus.

1.2 Taxonomic position of toadstools (Agaricales)

Toadstools are fungi. The Fungal Kingdom with over 40 000 species is quite distinct from the three other divisions of living organisms: the Plant Kingdom, the Animal Kingdom and the Kingdom of Bacteria. Fungi resemble green plants in being static and in having protoplasm encased in cell walls (so that only substances in solution can be absorbed), but differ fundamentally in their nutrition. Lacking chlorophyll they cannot photosynthesize their own food and, therefore, are forced to live either as parasites on other living organisms or as saprophytes on dead organic matter.

The principal classes of the Fungal Kingdom are shown in Table 1. Toadstools belong to Basidiomycetes, a class characterized by a special microscopic structure, the basidium, which bears its spores, usually four, externally (Fig. 1–1). A classification of Basidiomycetes is given in Table 2. Toadstools are members of the order Hymenomycetes. In this group the

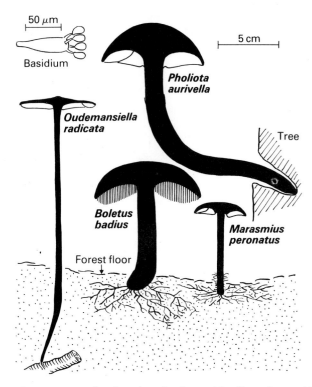

Fig. 1—1 Common woodland toadstools: three with gills and one with vertical tubes. *Boletus* and *Marasmius* are growing on the forest floor; *Oudemansiella* arises from a buried stick; *Pholiota* is growing from a tree trunk. All shown in vertical section to the same scale. Top left: basidium of *Oudemansiella*.

basidia, in their thousands or even millions, are crowded side by side to form extensive fertile surfaces (hymenia) displayed on conspicuous fruit-bodies or sporophores. The hymenium is exposed in such a way that the spores, which in Hymenomycetes are shot from the basidium to a distance of a fraction of a millimetre, are free to escape into the surrounding air. Together Hymenomycetes and Gasteromycetes include most of the large and conspicuous fungi so abundant in woods and on grassland in autumn. In Gasteromycetes (puff-balls, stinkhorns, bird's nest fungi) the spores are not actively discharged and the hymenium is not exposed. It has been suggested, however, that their ancestors were Hymenomycetes which, having lost the hymenomycete organization of spore liberation, were forced to develop mechanisms of dispersal along new and original lines.

Within Hymenomycetes there are many fungi that are not toadstools.

Table 1   Principal classes of the Fungi

Class	Approximate number of species	Characteristics
CHYTRIDIOMYCETES	600	Microscopic aquatic fungi
COMYCETES	550	Water moulds, and downy mildews of higher plants
ZYGOMYCETES	600	Pin moulds (e.g. *Mucor*)
ASCOMYCETES	15 000	Ascus containing (usually 8) ascospores
DEUTEROMYCETES	15 000	Conidial fungi lacking a normal sexual process
BASIDIOMYCETES	11 000	Basidium bearing basidio-spores (usually 4) externally

Table 2   Principal orders of Basidiomycetes

Order	Approximate number of species
UREDINALES (rusts)	5000
USTILAGINALES (smuts)	800
TREMELLALES (jelly fungi)	200
GASTEROMYCETES (puff-balls, stinkhorns, bird's nest fungi)	700
HYMENOMYCETES	
Aphyllophorales (bracket fungi and coral fungi)	1000
Agaricales (toadstools)	3300

These belong to Aphyllophorales·containing notably the leathery, corky and woody bracket fungi on dead, even living, branches and trunks of trees. The Agaricales are the true toadstools with many species. Indeed, in the British flora the number of species of toadstool is of the same order of magnitude as the number of flowering plants.

1.3   Names

Something should be said about names. A difficulty for the non-mycologist is that only a few toadstools have common, English, names which have general acceptance. It is, therefore, normally necessary to use the scientific names. For precision, the Latin name should be followed by the authority either in full or in a recognized abbreviation. Thus the Field Mushroom is *Agaricus campestris* Fries. However, in this booklet, for ease of reading, authorities for species have been omitted.

2 Toadstools: Form and Function

2.1 General features of toadstools

The greatest contribution by any single person to the biology of toadstools was made by A. H. R. Buller (1874–1944). His work was reported in 'Researches on Fungi' – some of the most original and readable volumes in the literature of mycology. We can best introduce this chapter by considering his beautiful illustration of the Horse Mushroom, *Agaricus arvensis* (Fig. 2–1). There are three phases: first, the long-lived feeding mycelium hidden in the ground deriving nourishment from the organic matter of the soil; secondly, the sporophore or fruit-body which lasts only a few days and is concerned with the production and liberation of spores; and thirdly, though normally invisible, the transient spore-cloud drifting away on the wind but continually recruiting myriads of spores newly liberated from the pileus.

At a later stage, more will be said about the vegetative mycelium, but now it is enough to remark that it consists of colourless hyphae converted by hyphal fusions into a three-dimensional network. It is not only a feeding system absorbing nutrients from the soil, it is also a conducting system, for in the production of a fruit-body above ground much material must be mobilized and concentrated at a certain point. It should be emphasized that the fruit-body is continuous with the vegetative mycelium and is really just a specialized part of it. Although looking so solid, a toadstool is built entirely of branched and interwoven hyphae and in this respect is completely different from the shoot of a green plant (Fig. 2–2).

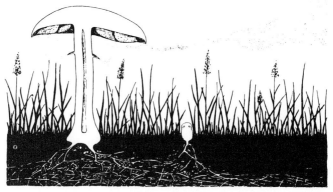

Fig. 2–1 *Agaricus arvensis*. Diagram of three phases: feeding mycelium in soil, sporophore, spore cloud. (After BULLER, 1909.)

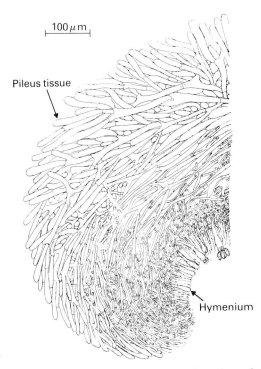

100 μm

Pileus tissue

Hymenium

Fig. 2–2   *Hygrophorus firmus.* Part of a longitudinal section of a fruit-body showing a small portion of the margin of the pileus. (After CORNER, E. J. H. (1936). *Trans. Br. mycol. Soc.,* **22**, 165.)

2.2   Structure of the fruit-body (sporophore)

The toadstool sporophore has an erect and rather rigid stipe crowned by a circular pileus and from this the gills (or tubes in *Boletus*) hang vertically. In some genera there are additional features (Fig. 2–3). There is commonly a ring round the stipe as in species of *Agaricus* and *Lepiota*. This represents the remains of a 'partial veil' which in the early (button) stage protects the developing gills in a gill-chamber. In most species of *Amanita* as well as a partial veil there is a 'universal veil' wrapping completely around the sporophore in the young state. When the toadstool expands this veil is left as a cup (volva) around the base of the stipe and sometimes also as torn fragments on the cap. The white spots on the red pileus of the Fly Agaric (*Amanita muscaria*) are remains of this universal veil. In the Tawny Grisette (*Amanita fulva*) there is no partial veil, but only a universal one that eventually remains as a basal volva. The veils, however, play little or no part in the functioning of the mature toadstool.

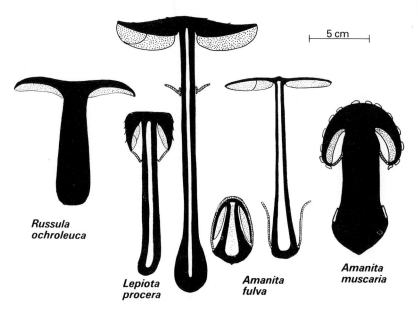

Fig. 2–3 Longitudinal sections of sporophores. *Russula* has no ring and no volva. *Lepiota* (two stages shown) ring only. *Amanita muscaria* (seen here in button stage) has a universal veil giving an adherent volva around base of stipe and white flakes on pileus; partial veil (still intact) will later provide a ring. *A.fulva* (two stages) has volva but no ring.

The fruit-body is, as we have seen, an apparatus concerned with the production and liberation of spores. Fungi reproduce by spores not seeds, although the academic distinction between the two was not made until the middle of the eighteenth century. Seeds and spores have the same reproductive function, but spores have a much simpler construction. In toadstools they are invariably unicellular, and, although varying considerably in size and shape, are mostly either spherical or ovoid with the length to breadth ratio not exceeding 4, and with the long axis not less than 4μm and not more than 20μm.

To explain the structure and function of a toadstool, one commonly encountered in beechwoods, *Oudemansiella radicata*, has been selected (Fig. 2–4). This species has a rather long stipe which is unusual in being prolonged downwards into the woodland soil as a tapering structure (pseudorhiza) that is in contact with buried wood in which the feeding mycelium ramifies. The rigid stipe is quite vertical. It is negatively geotropic, growing directly away from the centre of the earth. The cap is roughly horizontal. On its underside are the gills (lamellae) which are thin vertical plates slightly wedge-shape in section. They are covered by the

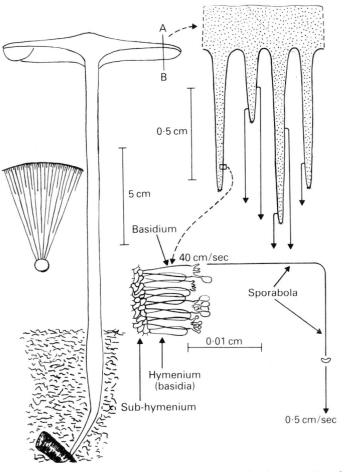

Fig. 2–4 *Oudemansiella radicata.* Sporophore in longitudinal section. Top right, tangential section at A—B. Bottom right, tiny part of hymenium at high power; trajectories of some spores indicated. Left, sector of underside of pileus to show gill arrangement.

spore-bearing surface or hymenium. This consists of millions of elongated basidia at all stages of development closely packed in what, in section, looks like a palisade. Most of them are horizontal. Occasional larger cells (cystidia) occur in the hymenium. These are also to be found at the free margin of the gill which is devoid of basidia, a general feature in toadstools. The basidia are bedded on the sub-hymenium. It must again be emphasized that the whole sporophore is of hyphal construction, but in the region of the subhymenium the packing is so close, and the interweaving of hyphae is so intimate, that in section it looks like the parenchymatous tissue of a flowering plant.

The basidium at an early stage is an elongated cell from the free end of which four curved outgrowths – sterigmata – develop. The tip of each sterigma swells to the full size of the mature basidiospore. This is disposed asymmetrically on its sterigma. The spore has a small basal projection (hilar appendix) and it is this that makes the liberated spore of a toadstool such a characteristic microscopic object. It is in the region of the hilar appendix that attachment to the sterigma occurs. In the discharged basidiospore the separation scar (hilum) is exceedingly small and can be demonstrated only with the high resolution of the scanning electron microscope.

2.3   Escape of spores from the sporophore

In *Oudemansiella radicata* the distance of discharge is about 0.02 cm. Each basidiospore is shot horizontally to this distance and then falls vertically. Buller has termed this trajectory a 'sporabola'. At first sight it looks improbable, being very different from the trajectory of a stone thrown horizontally. The sporabolic form is determined by the minute size of the basidiospore and the resulting major part played by the viscosity of the air. The sporabola can, in fact, easily be imitated by using a toy balloon. If this is struck horizontally from the top of a table, it travels rapidly forwards, quickly comes to a halt and then falls vertically. Again it is the master role played by the resistance of the air that determines the trajectory.

The horizontal limb of the sporabola is completed in a minute fraction of a second, and then in the vertical part the spore falls at a slow and steady rate of about 0.5 cm sec^{-1}. The falling spore does not accelerate like a dropped stone because of the overriding importance of air resistance for a microscopic particle.

In the main, spores are shot horizontally into the spaces between gills and then fall vertically in the still air that occurs there. Basidiospores are sticky and on contact with any surface become firmly stuck. For this reason, the distance between gills must be greater than the range of the basidium gun. Indeed, a certain margin of safety is necessary, and, in fact, opposing hymenial surfaces are rarely less then half a millimetre apart, more than twice the range of most basidia. Later we shall return to this question of the safe distance between gills.

Further, if the discharged spores are freely to escape from the pileus, not only must the gills be sufficiently far apart, but they must be vertical and stay so. If there is significant departure from the vertical, a discharged spore may either drop back on to the gill from which it came, or fall on to the opposite one (Fig. 2–5). We have seen that the stipe is negatively geotropic. This gives a rough vertical orientation to the gills hanging

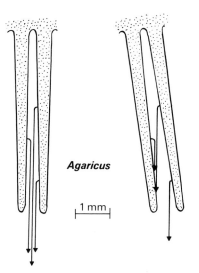

Fig. 2–5 *Agaricus campestris.* Part of a tangential vertical section of the pileus. Left: gills vertical. Right: gills 13° from vertical. Trajectories of some discharged spores are shown.

from the cap. But in addition to this coarse adjustment there is a fine one. Each individual gill is itself positively geotropic, and, if it departs from the vertical, growth movements occur until it is again in the vertical plane. The minute to minute verticality of the gills is ensured by the rigidity of the stipe which is a substantial column preventing the sporophore from swaying in a breeze.

It is evident that for the free fall of discharged spores a gill that is wedge-shaped, the normal condition in agarics, has an advantage over one with parallel sides, since it can deviate by a small angle from the vertical without spore-fall being impeded.

From a fair-sized toadstool basidiospores rain down at the rate of hundreds of thousands a minute. This enormous level is continued for the whole period, amounting usually to several days, of the life of a toadstool before it begins to rot. It is a relatively easy matter to demonstrate this rain of spores. To do this the stipe of any toadstool in good condition is removed and the pileus pinned in its natural attitude to a sheet of cork covering the mouth of a beaker of good quality glass or, better still, a museum jar with parallel sides. This is then placed in a dark-room and a strong parallel beam of light is passed through the beaker or jar at a level a few centimetres below the pileus. Through this beam the spores can be seen falling as a steady rain. Although far too small to be seen in their true form by the unaided eye, the spores, like motes in a sunbeam, scatter the light and are seen as minute falling stars.

2.4   Spore-prints

The abundance of spore production is seen also in the speed with which a spore-print is produced. The mycologist, in attempting to identify a toadstool often prepares a spore-print. This is done by cutting off the stipe of a fully expanded but fresh toadstool and placing the pileus, gills downwards, on a sheet of glass or on glossy paper. After a few hours the cap is removed and the spore-print is then visible, for by that time many millions of discharged spores have produced a system of radiating lines corresponding to the spaces between gills. The print may be white, cream, buff, brown, pink, purple or black. This colour is an important generic character.

That the spore-print is a picture of the spaces between gills is most readily appreciated in a species where the gills are rather distant and where the cap is often bell-shaped. In such a pileus the circumference can rest on the glass while the gills are free from contact with it (Fig. 2–6). The

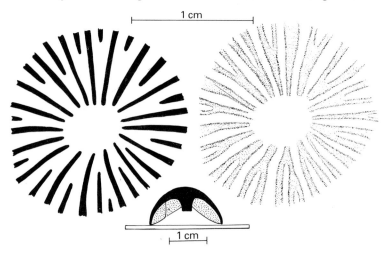

Fig. 2–6   *Laccaria laccata.* Below: sectional view of cap on glass sheet arranged to produce a spore-print. Left: worm's eye view of gill arrangement. Right: spore-print produced after three hours. In this the individual spores (many million) are not shown, but the density of spores is correctly indicated.

common *Laccaria laccata* is a good species to use in this connexion. The edges of the gills are without basidia so that in the print the gills are represented by ghosts free from spores. The only downward-projecting basidia contributing spores to the print are in the arches between adjacent gills. Since in *L. laccata* the distance separating opposite gill surfaces is 0.5–1.0 mm, and since the distance of discharge is only 0.1 mm, the deposit between two gills is not of uniform density. It tends to be thickest

along the edges where it has received the concentrated fire from a
considerable vertical area of gill, while in the middle it is much less dense
having received spores only from the arch uniting the two gills.

2.5   Ink-cap fungi

In most toadstools microscopic examination of any small area of gill
surface reveals basidia in all stages of development. However, the Ink-cap
fungi, species of *Coprinus*, have a different hymenial organization. One of
the most familiar of the larger species is *C. comatus*, the Shaggy Ink-cap
(Fig. 2–7). When a fruit-body that has just started to liberate spores is split

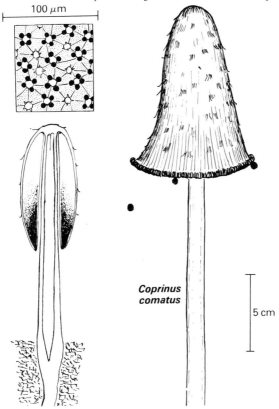

*Coprinus
comatus*

5 cm

Fig. 2–7 *Coprinus comatus*. Bottom left: longitudinal section before spore
liberation has started; gills white above grading to black below. Right: mature
autodigesting specimen producing droplets of ink. Top left: small part of black
gill surface where spore discharge is in progress. Spores have been shot from the
longer basidia, but are still attached to the shorter ones. The pavement of
paraphyses, in which the basidia are set, is stippled.

lengthwise, it is seen that each gill, the long axis of which is nearly vertical, is not of uniform colour. Instead it grades from white above through pink and brown to black below. This represents a gradient of development of the hymenium, the increasing pigmentation of the spores as they mature determining the colour of the gill. In any minute area of gill surface all basidia are at almost the same stage. Again, when a cross-section of a gill is examined (Fig. 2–8) the basidia are seen to be neatly spaced, sufficiently apart to allow them to operate freely, by sterile packing cells known as paraphyses. In surface view of the gill the paraphyses appear as a pavement in which the basidia are arranged in a regular pattern (Fig. 2–7). Basidia are of two different sizes; short and long. When discharge starts in a ripe region of the hymenium, the longer basidia shoot off their spores slightly in advance of the shorter ones giving a clear line of fire for the latter.

If a single gill, without any mounting fluid, is placed on a slide and viewed with the low power of the microscope, the pattern of basidial arrangement can easily be seen, each ripe basidium being represented by four black spores (Fig. 2–7).

The special feature of Ink-caps is autodigestion. As the black spores are discharged the edge of the gill becomes white, but this spore-free region is almost immediately removed by self digestion. This produces a black fluid

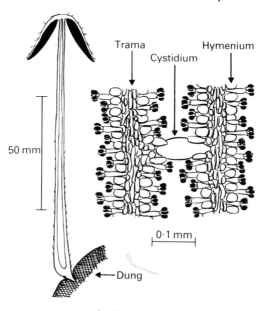

Fig. 2–8 *Coprinus cinereus.* Left: longitudinal section of sporophore. Right: sections of two gills with ripe basidia of two sizes interspersed with paraphyses; also cystidium. (Modified after BULLER, 1924.)

which, under damp conditions, flows down the inclined edges of the eroding gills and accumulates as an inky liquid around the margin of the cap which gradually gets smaller. The majority of the discharged spores escape in the normal way into the free air below the pileus, but a number drift into the ink.

Because the exhausted part of the gill is removed so quickly by autodigestion, the spores in *C. comatus* never have more than a fraction of a millimetre to fall between gill surfaces before emerging below the cap. Apparently associated with this is the fact that the gills are not geotropic as in other toadstools; exact verticality is no longer necessary. Also, there is no advantage in a gill that is wedge-shaped in section, and,.in fact, in the large species of *Coprinus* the gills have parallel sides.

Both in connexion with nutrition and with sex and genetics much attention will be given later to *C. cinereus* which commonly develops on horse dung (Fig. 2–8). A special feature of this species is the presence of scattered and very large cylindrical cells (cystidia) in the hymenium. These prop the gills sufficiently apart to allow the basidia to develop unimpeded in spite of the gills being so tightly packed together. As the cap opens umbrella-wise, the gills separate and the cystidia no longer bridge the gap. As in *C. comatus* there are long and short basidia.

2.6   Boletus

In addition to gill-bearing toadstools (agarics) there are boletes. These are fleshy toadstools in which the hymenium lines vertical tubes cemented together in honeycomb formation (Fig. 1–1). They are classified in the old genus *Boletus* which is now broken up by modern taxonomists into a number of genera. In all essentials the organization of the sporophore is like that of an agaric. Although the hymenial tubes, which must be wider than the distance of spore discharge, are, like gills, positively geotropic, their capacity to readjust is greatly restricted because of their union with neighbouring tubes.

2.7   Size and form in toadstools

Toadstools vary in size: in some the cap is only 0.2 cm across with a stipe a mere centimetre in length (e.g. in some species of *Marasmius*), while in others (e.g. the Parasol Mushroom, *Lepiota procera*) the pileus may be 20 cm wide and the stipe 25 cm long. Although the form of toadstools is relatively constant, there is considerable variation: the cap may be flat, hemispherical, conical or even funnel-shaped. Again, the amount of cap tissue in relation to the gills may vary greatly in different species. There is also much variety in texture: some fruit bodies are rather solid; others quite fragile. Nevertheless, the overall picture is one of general uniformity.

In any structure that varies in size but not in form, two-dimensional attributes increase as the square of the linear dimensions, whereas the three-dimensional features go up as the cube. Thus, in a toadstool-like object (Fig. 2–9) the volume, and therefore the weight, of the cap is determined by the cube, but the cross-section of the stipe, which supports that weight, is related to the square of the linear dimensions. Doubling these results in an eight-fold (2^3) increase in cap weight, whereas the cross-section of the stipe shows only a four-fold (2^2) increase.

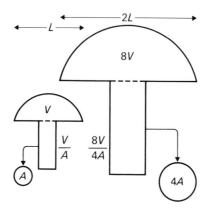

Fig. 2–9 Two toadstool-like structures of same form. One with linear dimension L; the other $2L$. In the smaller the ratio of cap volume to cross-section is V/A; in the larger $2V/A$.

We might expect, therefore, that the form of a toadstool would be somewhat related to its size; and that, as compared with a middle-sized species, large ones would tend to have stipes that were relatively thick, and smaller ones stipes that were relatively thin. An objective study (BOND, 1952), involving measurement of around a thousand species of agaric, has shown that the expected relationship between size and form certainly exists, although there are many individual departures from the rule.

Something should be said about the biological significance of the overall form of a toadstool. The umbrella shape is important because it ensures that the gill surfaces are sheltered from rain, for a hymenium of basidia is prevented from functioning, at least temporarily, if directly wetted. Nevertheless, the relative humidity of the air surrounding basidia must be at or near 100% and this is ensured by crowded gills or narrow hymenial tubes. Further, the stipe has two important functions: first, it supports the cap and gives the needed rigidity; secondly, it provides a space between the pileus and the ground so that falling spores stand a reasonable chance of being caught up in eddies and carried away on the wind.

2.8   Gill arrangement and the evolution of pores

Another geometrical question in toadstools is raised by gill arrangement. In most species the gills, which converge from the circumference of the pileus towards the stipe, are not all of the same length. There are often gills of three different sizes: long, medium and short (Fig. 2–4).

The distance between gills must exceed that to which basidiospores are shot (0.1–0.2 mm) and there must also be a margin of safety since no sporophore is quite rigid. There would thus seem to be a minimum safe distance separating hymenial surfaces. This is often around 0.5 mm.

Let us consider the situation in which all gills are of the same length. Hymenial surfaces would be at their closest nearest the stipe. Supposing they were there separated by the minimum safe distance, traced outwards there would come a position where this distance would be doubled. At this stage a new gill, extending outwards to the circumference, could safely be introduced, if we neglect the thickness of the gill itself; a factor for which allowance must be made but which does not affect the immediate argument. Nearer still to the margin of the pileus, depending on its diameter, a stage would be reached when separation between each long and each shorter gill would allow the introduction of another of still smaller size (Fig. 2–10). This is, indeed, the pattern in most toadstools.

It could be argued that the 'objective' of a toadstool is to produce as much hymenial surface, and therefore as many spores, as possible for a

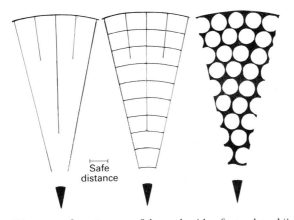

Safe distance

Fig. 2–10   Diagrams of a 25° sector of the underside of a toadstool (including a corresponding sector of the stipe shown as a black triangle). Left: agaric condition with hymenial surfaces at least the 'safe distance' apart. Middle: transitional state with radial gills joined by cross-connexions separated by radial distances equal to the 'safe distance'. Right: bolete condition with hymenial pores the 'safe distance' in diameter. Total length of hymenium on right (pores) is 50% greater than on left (gills). (It should be noted that each gill has hymenium on both surfaces.)

given expenditure of energy on supporting tissue of cap and stipe. The development of gills and pores itself represents a means of increasing hymenial surface with economical expenditure on supporting tissue. Having gills of different length adds considerably to the area of hymenium that can be efficiently organized below the cap. However, there is still a certain wastage of space since no new gill can be introduced until the separating distance becomes double the safe one. Tangential cross-connexions between gills, provided they are separated in the radial direction by the safe distance, would give considerable extra surface for the display of basidia. Such cross-partitioning is, perhaps, the first step towards a *Boletus*-type sporophore (Fig. 2–10). In Britain, most toadstools are either gill-bearing agarics or thorough-going boletes. However, in tropical forests many more intermediate types are to be seen. It is generally considered that the bolete kind of sporophore has arisen from the agaric as a result of increasing development of cross-connexions between gills. Further, there is strong evidence that this has happened on more than one occasion in toadstool evolution.

2.9   Spore production and the problem of wastage

As we have seen, spore production by a toadstool is prodigious. Measurement of this output is quite simple. The most usual method is to allow spores falling from a pileus to collect in a beaker over a certain time. These can then be suspended in a known volume of water and their number estimated with the aid of a haemacytometer. Buller found that a Field Mushroom having a cap 8 cm across liberated spores at an average rate of 600 000 a minute during the spore-fall period that lasted for about two days.

A different approach to the calculation of basidiospore output is possible in the Ink-caps. In *Coprinus comatus*, for example, we have seen that any small area produces only one crop of basidia (Fig. 2–7). By examining a gill in surface view under the microscope it is, therefore, simple to count the number of basidiospores in a small defined area. In *C. comatus* the gills are all of the same size. Knowing the area of a single gill and their number, spore production of the whole sporophore can be accurately calculated. Buller found that for a large specimen this was 5 240 000 000. Since the spore-fall is spread over a period of about 48 hours, the mean rate of liberation is 1 600 000 per minute, a figure of the same order of magnitude as that for the Field Mushroom.

This immense output of spores raises the question of wastage. The chances against an individual spore succeeding in its reproductive function, by giving rise to a new productive mycelium, are astronomically great. It seems likely that the opportunities for successful establishment are few and far between, and, therefore, in order to seize these when and where they arise, this enormous output may be essential. Further, as will be shown later, in most species a single spore is not capable of establishing a new fruiting mycelium on its own. The monokaryotic mycelium which it can intitiate must unite in due course with one of compatible mating type if toadstools are to be produced. This would seem to mean that not only must a spore come to rest in the right place under the right conditions, but it must fall beside or very close to an appropriate partner. This greatly steps up the amount of wastage that is inevitable under a system of random scattering.

Dispersal seems vital to the survival of a species by allowing it to seize the opportunities, often very infrequent, to establish new individuals and so maintain, and perhaps gradually extend, the population. It also permits the scatter of genetic variability, as it arises by chance mutation, throughout the population, thus contributing to to the genetic flexibility of the species on which its survival may ultimately depend.

3 The Basidium as a Spore-gun

3.1 Introduction

A large number of fungi liberate their spores actively and in most of these the mechanism of discharge is clearly understood. However, in toadstools and their allies the position is quite different. Although the series of visible events associated with the projection of basidiospores has been known in detail for over half a century, there is still no completely acceptable explanation of how the basidium operates as a spore-gun. It is this problem that is discussed in the present chapter, and in so doing it will be necessary to refer to spore discharge in some other fungi unrelated to toadstools.

3.2 Development of the basidium

First, it is important to have a detailed picture of the basidium (Fig. 3–1). Initially it is a club-shaped cell fully charged with granular protoplasm. Then a clear, sap-filled vacuole arises near its base. This starts to enlarge and, at about the same time, the sterigmata grow out from the top of the basidium. The tips of these then begin to swell into spores. The vacuole continues to enlarge, seeming to act almost as a piston forcing most of the protoplasm through the sterigmata, which are exceedingly narrow tubes, into the swelling spores (Fig. 3–1b). When the process is complete, it is not clear whether there is a cross-wall at the narrow junction of sterigma and spore. This is on such a small scale that the problem cannot be settled by light microscopy. The few observations that have been made with the electron microscope on ultra-thin sections through the region of attachment of nearly ripe spores, indicate that at maturity there is at least protoplasmic separation of sterigma and spore (Fig. 3–2). A basic difficulty is that, on preparing material for sectioning, really ripe spores invariably become detached from their sterigmata.

The mature basidiospore is poised asymmetrically on its sterigma, attachment being in the region of the hilar appendix. On the liberated basidiospore the actual separation scar (hilum) is about 0.2 μm across. It is too small to be seen under the light microscope, a limitation imposed by the wavelength of light, but has been studied extensively in discharged basidiospores with the aid of the electron microscope.

The asymmetrical perching of the spore on its sterigma is achieved in a characteristic manner (Fig. 3–1a). The incipient basidiospore is a symmetrical swelling of the tip of the sterigma. It then blows out laterally leaving the remaining part unexpanded as the hilar appendix.

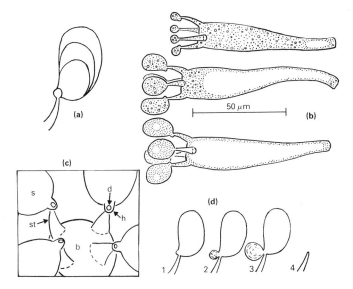

Fig. 3–1 *Oudemansiella radicata.* (a) Four superimposed stages in growth of the spore; the initial spore-primordium is spherical. (b) Three basidia of increasing age. (c) Oblique top view of basidium (b) showing discoid area (d) on hilar appendix (h) of spore (s) borne on a sterigma (st). (Copied from a scanning electron micrograph supplied by Dr. T. Young.) (d) Stages (1–4) in basidiospore discharge; about 30 seconds separate stages 1 and 4. (The scale relates only to (b).)

3.3   Discharge of basidiospores

Just before discharge what appears to be a minute droplet, but may rather be a gas-filled bubble or blister, suddenly appears on the hilar appendix close to the hilum, grows in the course of a few seconds to a definite size, but smaller than the spore itself, and then the spore is shot away. Recent studies of the hymenium with the scanning electron microscope indicate that there is a discoid area on the hilar appendix (Fig. 3–1c). It is probably from this region that the drop (or bubble) arises. Electron-microscopic studies of *Coprinus cinereus* have shown that a special organelle (hilar appendix body) is associated with the plasmalemma of the basidiospore in the region of the hilar appendix. It is tempting to suggest that this body is in some way involved in drop (bubble) production.

It is a feature of the basidium in toadstools that the four spores are normally discharged in succession with a few seconds, or even minutes, elapsing between the liberation of sister spores (Fig. 3–3). Immediately following discharge of a spore, its sterigma seems to be unaltered in size

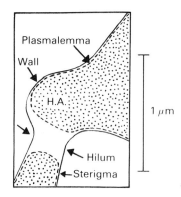

Fig. 3–2 *Lentinus edodes*. Section through junction of sterigma and basidiospore as seen with the electron microscope. The whole of the hilar appendix is shown (H.A.), but only a small part of the rest of the basidiospore. Protoplasm is indicated by dotting, but the contained organelles are not represented. The plasmalemma is shown by an interrupted line and the outer layer of the cell wall by a continuous one. The future position of separation that produces the hilum is indicated by a pair of arrows. (Based on an electron micrograph by NAKAI, Y. (1975). In: *Rept. Tottori Mycol. Inst. (Japan)*, 12, 41–6.)

and form and no fluid is to be seen on the vacated tip nor does any ooze from it subsequently. Obviously if a drop is exuded at the hilar appendix it is carried away with the discharged spore.

When discharge is occurring the basidium is a turgid cell and its wall is lined by a thin layer of protoplasm, the bulk of the basidium being taken up with a large sap-vacuole. At this stage, most of the granular protoplasm originally present has been driven into the spores. Following discharge of the fourth spore, the basidium slowly disintegrates.

3·4 Mechanism of discharge

We now come to the problem of the mechanism of discharge. Three of the current ideas rest on comparison with known behaviour in other organisms. A water-squirting gun may be involved as in *Pilobolus*; the mechanism may depend on sudden rounding-off of a turgid spore as in *Entomophthora*; or the bursting of an air-blister on the spore may be responsible for jerking it from the sterigma, as in the slime-mould *Schizoplasmodium*. To clarify these possibilities, the discharge of spores in these three organisms will be briefly considered.

Pilobolus (Fig. 3–4) is a mucoraceous mould developing regularly on horse droppings and on other herbivore dung. Each sporangiophore is a large turgid cell consisting of a basal bulb in the dung and an erect stalk leading to an ovoid crystal bulb capped by a black sporangium. The

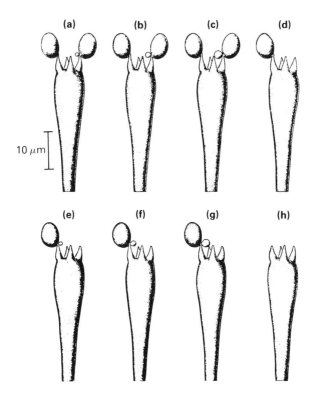

Fig. 3–3 *Agaricus campestris*. Successive stages (a–h) in the discharge of the third and fourth spores from a basidium. A few seconds separate a and d; and also e and h: but several minutes separate d and e. (After BULLER, 1922.)

turgid sporangiophore bursts along a pre-determined circular line of weakness just below the sporangium and immediately its stretched wall contracts squirting out the liquid contents with the sporangium on top to a distance of up to two metres.

It is just possible that basidiospore discharge is of this nature, but on a microscopic scale. However, there are great difficulties. The sterigma seems unchanged immediately after the spore has been shot off, and appears to be closed. There is no exudation of fluid from the vacated sterigma which might be expected were it open. Indeed, if it were open at the instant of discharge almost immediate self-sealing would be necessary to conserve the hydrostatic pressure in the basidium for discharge of the next spore. It is difficult to see how this could occur. Again, a water-squirting theory does not bring into the picture the process of drop (or bubble) development from the base of the basidiospore that heralds liberation.

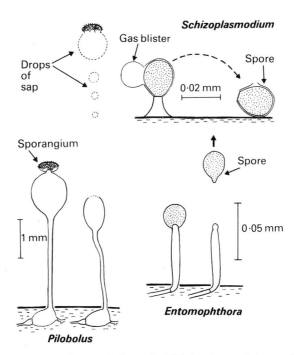

Fig. 3–4 Diagrams of spore discharge in *Pilobolus*, *Entomophthora* and *Schizoplasmodium*. In *Schizoplasmodium* a spore is shown on its stalk with lateral gas blister; when this bursts the spore is thrown to one side. (Based on photographs and descriptions by OLIVE and STOIANOVITCH, 1966.)

Another theory is that discharge of the basidiospore is like conidium release in *Entomophthora*, species of which parasitize insects. *E. coronata* is particularly easy to study because it grows well in pure culture on simple laboratory media. From the mycelium in the nutrient substratum simple erect conidiophores grow into the air each terminated by a single large, and nearly spherical, conidium. This is separated from the conidiophore by a curved cross-wall which bulges into the conidium. The separating wall is a two-ply structure, one layer belonging to the conidiophore, the other to the conidium. The conidium, like the conidiophore, is a turgid living cell and as such tends to push out the re-entrant region where the tip of the conidiophore pokes into it. To this tense situation relief suddenly comes: the re-entrant part springs out and the conidium in consequence leaps off the conidiophore to a distance of several centimetres.

If basidiospore discharge is comparable to that of the conidium of *Entomophthora*, it would be necessary for a two-ply wall to exist at maturity where sterigma and basidiospore meet; and the evidence for this is meagre. It is, however, to be noted that there is no need for the tip of the sterigma to bulge into the spore; it would be sufficient if there were just a flat zone of contact. In this minute region spore and sterigma, both in a turgid condition, would strain to become convex and a situation of tension would exist. If this were suddenly relieved, violent spore discharge might occur on the *Entomophthora* model. As with the previous theory, however, this takes no account of the phenomenon of drop (bubble) development near the base of the spore just before discharge.

A third idea depends on the view that what forms near the base of the basidiospore prior to discharge is a gas-filled bubble or blister and not a droplet. It is suggested that the bursting of this is responsible for active spore liberation. In this connexion it is important to note that merely by microscopic examination of a basidium in its normal situation surrounded by air, it seems impossible to determine whether it is a droplet or a bubble that develops on the hilar appendix of the spore.

The revolutionary bubble-bursting idea was advanced (OLIVE and STOIANOVITCH, 1966) following the discovery that a mechanism of this kind does occur in *Schizoplasmodium*, a minute slime-mould.

Rather recently a new group (Protostelida) of slime-moulds (Mycetozoa) has come to light. Members of the group were earlier overlooked, probably because of their small size. In most species of Protostelida a single spore is borne on an erect stalk. *Schizoplasmodium cavostelioides* belongs to this group and its spore is violently discharged (Fig. 3–4). The spore-wall, though thin, is two-ply. At maturity gas develops between the two layers to form a spherical lateral blister about as large as the spore itself. This eventually bursts and the small explosion jerks the spore from its stalk. That the contents of the blister are gaseous is clear when a fully mature specimen is mounted in water.

The discovery of *Schizoplasmodium* with its bubble-bursting mechanism of discharge naturally led to the suggestion that the same thing happens in basidiospore release. However, because the basidiospore is smaller and because it is so loosely perched on its sterigma at the moment of liberation, it is nearly impossible to mount in water a specimen with its basal bubble (present only for a few seconds) and so confirm the gaseous nature of its contents.

A problem for the bubble-bursting theory is the trajectory of the basidiospore. It seems to be shot outwards more or less in line with the longitudinal axis of the basidium. A bursting blister would, however, tend to knock it sideways. Further, if such a blister were to rupture, we might reasonably expect to see, on liberated basidiospores viewed with the scanning electron microscope, remnants of a torn membrane in the region of the hilar appendix. Basidiospores of many species have now been examined in this way and such torn membranes have not been observed.

These difficulties appear, however, to be surmountable. The gas may be pictured as being produced in the hilar appendix between the outer and inner layers of the spore-wall; the outer elastic one being greatly stretched in the blister. When rupture occurs at the hilum, the stretched wall of the blister is able to contract, driving a jet of gas through the hilar breach between the two layers of the wall. Such a jet directed backwards might carry the spore along the observed trajectory and there would be no ruptured membrane on the spore in addition to the hilum (Fig. 3–5).

A further line of evidence supports the gas-blister theory. This comes from a study of spore discharge from toadstools subjected to very high (around 50 atmospheres) pressures in a specially designed pressure chamber. Under these conditions basidiospore discharge ceases, to be resumed when pressure returns to its normal level (INGOLD, 1969). However, fungi discharging their spores by water-squirting (e.g. *Sordaria*, an ascomycete) or by a rounding-off mechanism (e.g. *Entomophthora*) shoot their spores quite freely under such high external pressure. In both these mechanisms no interference with spore discharge would be expected as the hydrostatic pressure would simply become equalized throughout the system. However, if for discharge to occur a gas bubble has to be blown against a pressure of 50 atmospheres, the expectation is quite different. It might then be expected that discharge would be stopped or greatly impeded.

It should be said that a spore poised asymmetrically on a fine sterigma and discharged therefrom following drop (bubble) extrusion from a basal projection is referred to as a 'ballistospore'. Not all basidiospores are ballistospores; the basidiospores of Gasteromycetes are not shot from

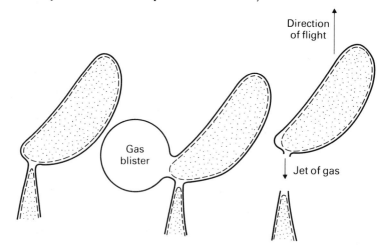

Fig. 3–5   Diagram of basidiospore discharge on the assumption that a gas blister is produced at the base of the spore and that the gas escapes through the ruptured hilum. (Based on the ideas of MOORE, R. T. (1966). *Science, N. Y.*, **154**, 424.)

their sterigmata, but the basidiospores of all toadstools are ballistospores. Further, not all ballistospores are basidiospores. The aerial spores of the extremely common 'mirror-image yeasts' (belonging to the Sporobolomycetaceae) are ballistospores. When colonies of *Sporobolomyces* are grown on agar in petri dishes kept in an inverted position, mirror pictures of the colonies are precisely reproduced on the inside of the lid by deposits of discharged ballistospores. On the basis that the ballistopore is a basidiomycete character, mycologists regard Sporobolomycetaceae as a family of the Basidiomycetes. Because they are easily manipulated in culture, mirror-picture yeasts have been used in attempts to understand the mechanism of ballistospore discharge.

When the bubble-bursting theory of discharge was first advanced, it seemed to many mycologists that the long-standing problem had at last been solved. However, there are real difficulties in accepting this theory principally because of some rather good evidence that the discharged spore is, indeed, accompanied by liquid that could represent an extruded drop. For example, MÜLLER (1954) filmed the process of ballistospore discharge in *Sporobolomyces*. In one instance the spore with its basal drop (or bubble) fully-developed was present in one frame of the film, and in the next, a sixty-fourth of a second later, the spore had landed nearby and appeared to be accompanied by fluid roughly equivalent to the drop. Some of Buller's observations also recorded liquid associated with basidiospores immediately after their discharge.

Another technique that has been brought to bear on the ballistospore problem and using *Sporobolomyces* is that of microdissection (VAN NIEL, GARNER and COHEN, 1972). When the tip of a microdissection needle manipulated under the high-power objective, makes contact with a ballistospore on its aerial sterigma, the two adhere firmly, for the surface of the spore is sticky. By skilful probing it was found that at first the fully-grown spore is relatively firmly attached to the sterigma. However, some time before discharge is due to occur, attachment becomes so greatly weakened that the ballistospore seems to be no longer actually attached, but merely perched on the sterigma. Following contact with the tip of the microdissection needly, such a spore could readily be removed from its sterigma to a position a few micrometres away, with continuous observation being maintained. In due course a bubble (drop) was seen to exude from the hilar appendix of the freed spore. Then associated with the apparent explosion of the bubble, there was a sudden shift of the spore on the needle (Fig. 3–6). Van Niel and his co-workers concluded from certain other observations that a bubble was involved rather than a drop. However, experiments, using a micropipette in place of a microdissection needle, suggested that the bubble was accompanied by some liquid.

If a gas bubble or blister is produced, there remains the question of the nature of the gas and how it is produced. No answer can yet be given.

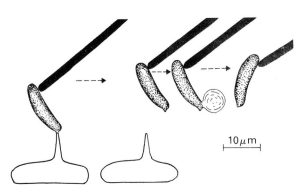

10μm

Fig. 3–6 *Sporobolomyces*. Highly diagrammatic picture of findings of VAN NIEL, GARNER and COHEN (1972). A vegetative yeast cell has produced an aerial sterigma bearing a ballistospore now loosely attached. The ballistospore has then been touched by the tip of the microdissection needle and removed from the sterigma. Then the bubble has formed and has finally burst displacing the spore about its attachment to the needle.

However, we have seen that gas formation does occur in *Schizoplasmodium*. Another example is to be seen in the pollen grain of pine in which there are two lateral gas bladders between outer and inner layers of the wall.

The bubble-bursting theory of basidiospore discharge can be illustrated in a model (Fig. 3–7). Two toy balloons are involved. One represents the spore and rests loosely on an artificial sterigma; a jam-jar being suitable. The second, stuck to the first, represents the gas blister. This can conveniently rest freely in the ring of a retort-stand. At the desired moment the neck of the blister-balloon is cut off with sharp scissors, and the spore balloon flies into the air. If the gas-blister theory is the right one, then the basidiospore is, as it were, powered by its own little jet engine.

3.5 Other theories of ballistospore discharge

For each of the three theories of ballistospore discharge so far discussed, it is possible to point to an organism in which the kind of discharge envisaged actually occurs. However, there are other possibilities.

One that deserves further study is the possibility that discharge is due to electrostatic repulsion. Basidiospores liberated into the air habitually carry static charges. It has been suggested that charged spores perched loosely on their sterigmata might be violently repelled therefrom by a similar charge on the gill.

Another possibility is that the surface energy of a drop exuded at the

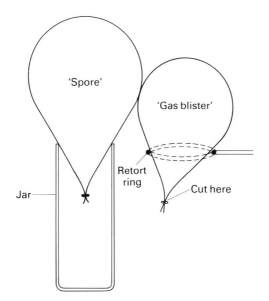

Fig. 3–7 Model of ballistospore discharge using two balloons. The model works when the neck of the 'gas blister' balloon is instantaneously cut off at the point indicated.

hilar appendix might be used in spore release. It seems that more than enough of this energy to effect discharge is availabe, but it is hard to see how this could be mobilized.

The fact remains that the problem of the mechanism of ballistospore discharge still remains unsolved.

4 Sex and Genetics in Toadstools

4.1 Monokaryons and dikaryons

The genetics of fungi is a large and complex study and there are several substantial textbooks dealing with this subject alone. What is attempted in this chapter is a brief outline to bring the genetical and cytological events into relationship with other aspects of the nature of toadstools. Although the volume of knowledge on toadstool genetics is considerable, the number of species studied has been limited. *Coprinus cinereus* has been most fully investigated largely because it grows quickly, fruits readily and has spores that are easy to germinate. We shall, therefore, concentrate on this fungus and only later consider how far what is known about it also holds for other agarics.

Consideration of a life-cycle can start at any point, but it is convenient to begin with the spore. This is haploid. If a colony of *C. cinereus* in pure culture on nutrient agar, or on sterilized horse dung, is grown from a single basidiospore, it fails to fruit. The mycelium of branched, septate hyphae derived from the spore is composed of uni-nucleate cells each with a haploid nucleus. It is a monokaryotic mycelium, more briefly termed a monokaryon. If a number of single-spore colonies are produced from one and the same fruit-body, these, although normally indistinguishable from one another, can be sorted into four types (I, II, III, IV) on the basis of their reactions with one another. If I and II are grown together in the same petri dish, where they meet union occurs and a dikaryotic mycelium (dikaryon) of bi-nucleate cells develops. In uniting to produce a dikaryon they are said to be compatible. Similarly III and IV are compatible. However, no other combination results in a dikaryon. It is normally only from a dikaryotic mycelium that sporophores are produced.

It is possible to isolate the four spores of a single basidium and grow them separately. When the mating potentialities of the colonies from such basidiospores are investigated, it is found that on a single basidium the four spores are (1) two of type I and two of type II; or (2) two of type III and two of IV; or (3) one of each of the four types. In other words, from the point of view of the mating type of the spores, there are three kinds of basidium on any one fruit-body. We shall deal with the explanation of this matter soon, but first it is necessary to consider what happens when two compatible monokaryons meet.

The situation is represented in an extremely diagrammatic manner in Fig. 4–1. When compatible mycelia meet, hyphal unions occur and, as a result, nuclei of the two types come to lie in the same cell. However, they do not fuse, but the dikaryotic cell gives rise to a dikaryotic mycelium in

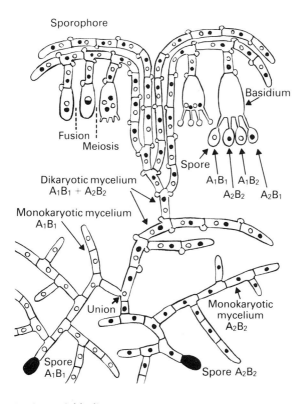

Fig. 4–1 *Coprinus.* Highly diagrammatic representation of the union (lower part of figure) of two compatible mycelia (A₁B₁ and A₂B₂) without clamp-connexions to form a dikaryotic mycelium (A₁B₁ + A₂B₂) with clamps giving a sporophore (crudely suggested). Nuclear fusion in the young basidium is followed by meiosis and a basidium is shown with four kinds of basidiospore.

which each cell has two nuclei. These remain of the two original mating-types as the result of a curious kind of cell division that produces clamp-connexions at the septa. The dikaryotic mycelium is recognizable by these clamps.

When the monokaryons meet, not only are there hyphal fusions with the immediate development of dikaryotic cells, but there is also nuclear migration from one haploid mycelium throughout the other. Thus, in the situation illustrated in Fig. 4–2, nuclei migrate from one monokaryon into the other (and *vice versa*) passing apparently from cell to cell. The nuclei probably divide as they go and in a surprisingly short time the colonies are dikaryotized so that, all around the growing periphery of both colonies, mycelium with clamp-connexions is produced.

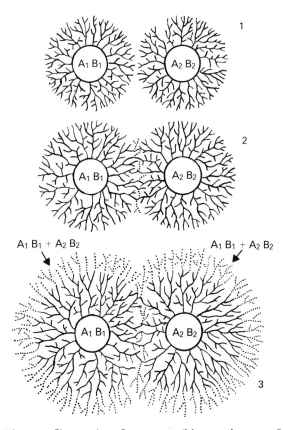

Fig. 4–2 Diagram of interaction of two compatible monokaryons of *Coprinus* on agar. (1) Two colonies 5 days' old (having developed from small central inocula) are about to make contact. (2) A day later they have met and a little dikaryotic mycelium (dotted) has developed. (3) After a further 1–2 days nuclear migration has occurred and, around each of the original colonies of unclamped mycelium, a growing fringe of clamped dikaryotic hyphae (dotted) has developed.

The radial growth of each monokaryon at 20°C is 2–3 mm a day, but the speed of migration of the nuclei is around 20 mm a day. There is no clear understanding of the mechanism of this rapid migration. It seems almost as if the nuclei, rather like amoebae, have independent power of movement. There is a further problem, namely of how the nuclei manage to pass from cell to cell. In the ascomycete mycelium with each cross-wall perforated by a simple pore, passage of nuclei from cell to cell presents no great difficulty. However, in toadstools and other Basidiomycetes the complex pore, which will be described shortly, presents a barrier that has to be broken down before a nucleus can pass. It seems that this simplification does, in fact, occur. There is, however, much that needs clarification in this rapid passage of nuclei through the mycelium.

4.2   Clamp-connexions and dolipores

In the long narrow cell of a dikaryotic hypha the two nuclei do not normally lie side by side, but one is in advance of the other. If following division of the two nuclei, cross-walls were formed dividing the hypha into binucleate cells, it is evident, since growth is apical and only the end cell divides, that the hypha would almost immediately have nuclei of only one genetic type (Fig. 4–3b). The dikaryotic situation is normally maintained by a complex process of cell division involving the production of a clamp-connexion.

Clamp formation is illustrated in Fig. 4–3. A small lateral outgrowth of

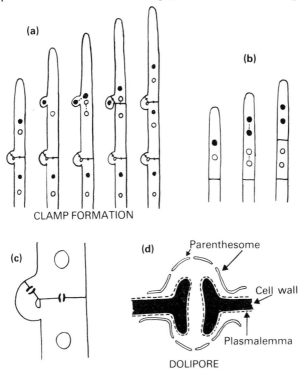

Fig. 4–3   Diagram of clamps and dolipores in *Coprinus*. Haploid nuclei of one type (say A_1B_1 – o) and other compatible type (A_2B_2 – ●). (a) Nuclear and cell division with formation of clamps. (b) Type of division that would break up the dikaryotic pair. (c) Region of clamp showing dolipores in cross-walls. (d) Details of single dolipore.

the apical cell is formed and into this the upper of the two nuclei passes. Both now divide. One daughter of the upper nucleus remains in the outgrowth, the other shunting back into the apical cell. Cross-walls now arise between both pairs of daughter nuclei. The result is a bi-nucleate apical cell, a small uni-nucleate lateral one and a uni-nucleate penultimate one. The tip of the outgrowth now bends backwards, fuses with the top of the penultimate cell and discharges its nucleus into that cell. Thus the clamp-connexion (or clamp) is formed. By this mechanism the two nuclei in each cell remain descendants of the two of different, but compatible, mating-type that originally paired when monokaryons met.

The highly diagrammatic view of the mycelium of a toadstool so far represented may be corrected, perhaps, by reference to Fig. 4–4 which shows small portions of both the monokaryon and the dikaryon of *C. cinereus*.

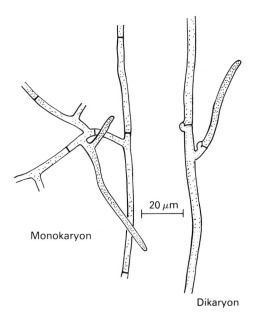

Monokaryon

20 μm

Dikaryon

Fig. 4–4 *Coprinus cinereus.* Small portion of monokaryon and of dikaryon. Nuclei are not visible in these living hyphae; staining is necessary if they are to be seen.

We may now consider the structure of the dolipore in the cross-wall of the agaric mycelium as seen in ultra-thin sections under the electron microscope (Fig. 4–3d). It is in the form of an open barrel with each end covered by a structure (parenthesome) composed of apparently firm but perforated double membrane looking rather like a domestic colander. It seems that this allows the smaller protoplasmic organelles to flow from cell to cell, a process often observable under the high power of the light microscope, but normally prevents the passage of nuclei.

4·3   Cytology of the basidium

It has already been seen that the sporophore is made up of coherent and interwoven hyphae, and, indeed, is an aerial extension of the mycelium that ramifies in the nutrient substratum. The hyphae of the sporophore are dikaryotic, the cells having clamps at the septa. In the gills the basidia are formed and each starts as a dikaryotic cell with a basal clamp (Fig. 4–5). Then the two nuclei of the young basidium fuse. Thus the nuclear association, which began when compatible monokaryons met, is completed by fusion in the basidium. It becomes diploid. It should, however, be emphasized that from the point of view of genetics the pair of nuclei of a dikaryon behaves like a diploid nucleus, and the characteristics of the sporophore are, as in a true diploid, determined by the dominant alleles of the pair of haploid nuclei.

No sooner is the diploid nucleus formed in the young basidium than it undergoes the two successive divisions that together constitute meiosis. Since there are two divisions of the nucleus with one replication of the chromosomes, the four resulting nuclei are haploid. Thus, although the dikaryotic condition lasts for a considerable time in the life-cycle of a toadstool, the diploid state is of extremely short duration.

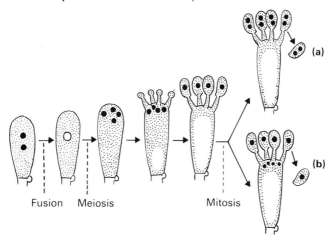

Fusion   Meiosis   Mitosis

Fig. 4–5 Cytology of the basidium. Usually the haploid nucleus in the basidiospore undergoes a further mitosis and the spore is shed in the bi-nucleate condition (a); but in some species one haploid nucleus migrates back into the basidium and there degenerates (b). Two less usual patterns of behaviour are not figured.

Around the time of meiosis the sterigmata begin to sprout from the top of the basidium and their apices swell into basidiospores. In most toadstools, when the spores have reached their full size, a haploid nucleus migrates into each through the narrow tube that is the sterigma. In the spore the nucleus almost always undergoes a mitotic division. In most species the resulting two nuclei remain in the basidiospore which is liberated in the bi-nucleate condition. However, in others, one of the two daughter nuclei produced by mitosis in the spore migrates back through the sterigma into the basidium (Fig. 4–5).

4·4 Genetics of mating

We must now consider the genetics of the mating situation. For any one sporophore the ability of monokaryons derived from it to mate appears to be conditioned by two pairs of alleles which can be designated A_1 and A_2, and B_1 and B_2. The A and B genes apparently occur on different chromosomes indicated by their independent segregation in basidiospore formation. The four monokaryons produced by the germination of basidiospores are A_1B_1, A_2B_2, A_1B_2 and A_2B_1 since the haploid nucleus can carry only one of each pair of alleles. These are the types earlier designated I, II, III and IV. A_1B_1 is compatible with A_2B_2 and A_1B_2 with A_2B_1, but other combinations are incompatible. The rule seems to be that for compatibility the alleles at the A locus must be different; and those at the B locus must also be different. The two dikaryons with clamp-connexions that can be formed are $A_1B_1 + A_2B_2$ and $A_1B_2 + A_2B_1$. In both cases the diploid nucleus is $A_1A_2B_1B_2$. At meiosis there is segregation and basidiospores of only four mating types result. Whether a basidium produces basidiospores of only two types or whether it bears all four depends on whether separation of the alleles occurs at the first or at the second division of meiosis (Fig. 4–6).

There is a further complication in the story. It is found that if the four monokaryons derived from a particular sporophore are tested against any single monokaryon from a sporophore some distance away (and therefore likely to be the product of a different dikaryotic mycelium), they are usually all compatible with this, or with any other monokaryon from the second fruit-body. The explanation appears to be that, considering the whole population of the species, at the A locus and also at the B locus there is not just a pair of alleles, but a group – namely A_1, A_2, A_3, A_4 . . . . . . and B_1, B_2, B_3, B_4 . . . . However, the diploid nucleus in the young basidium can carry only two alleles from each group, and consequently, so far as mating type is concerned, the sporophore formed on a given dikaryon can produce only four types of basidiospore. These, when the diploid condition is $A_1A_2B_1B_2$, are A_1B_1, A_2B_2, A_1B_2 and A_2B_1; while in a sporophore in which the young basidia have the composition $A_5A_8B_3B_7$, the basidiospores are A_5B_3, A_8B_7, A_5B_7 and A_8B_3. In accordance

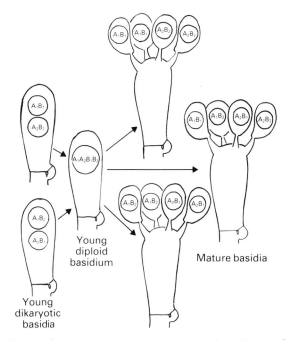

Fig. 4–6 *Coprinus cinereus.* Mating-type segregation in basidiospore formation.

with the rule that for compatibility the alleles at each of the two loci must be different, any of the monokaryons from the second sporophore is compatible with all those from the first. Genetic analysis suggests that in *C. cinereus* there are some 160 alleles of the A gene and about half that number of the B gene.

There is evidence that the B gene is concerned with nuclear migration between pairing monokaryons, and the A gene with the formation of clamp-connexions.

The situation in which mating, or sexual reaction, depends on two independent genes is unusual amongst living organisms. Normally only one is concerned. Indeed, this is the situation in a minority of toadstools notably in the Fairy-ring Fungus, *Marasmius oreades*. Here only A alleles are involved and a fruit-body produces basidiospores of two genetic types from the point of view of mating. Again there are a few agarics in which fruit-bodies are regularly produced on the mycelium derived from the germination of a single haploid basidiospore. A dikaryon soon becomes established with paired nuclei of identical genetic constitution. An example is *Coprinus sterquilinus*.

The situation in the Cultivated Mushroom, *Agaricus bisporus*, is anomalous. As in *C. sterquilinus*, a fruiting mycelium results from the germination of a single spore. Nevertheless, it appears that a single mating-type gene is involved as in *M. oreades* with multiple alleles. The young basidium has two nuclei: one with the A_1 allelle and the other with A_2. The fusion nucleus has the constitution A_1A_2. Meiosis follows giving four nuclei: A_1, A_1, A_2 and A_2. In *A. bisporus* the basidium is unusual in normally producing only two spores. What appears to happen is that both of the spores of the basidium receives an A_1 and an A_2 nucleus. Hence, on germination a mycelium is formed which, having the two mating-type alleles, has the potential to fruit. Analysis of the situation is possible because occasionally four-spored basidia are produced, each spore receiving a haploid nucleus. With great skill, spores from a few of these have been isolated and germinated to give single-spore cultures. These fail to fruit, but belong to two types so that when compatible monokaryons are mated, a fruiting mycelium results. Since genes other than those concerned with mating segregate at meiosis, the raising of single-spore cultures from four-spored basidia gives the breeder a chance to develop new strains of Cultivated Mushroom by genetic re-combination.

We have seen that, by the process of clamp-connexion formation, the two genetic types of nuclei are maintained in each cell of the dikaryon. However, there are quite a number of toadstools that are devoid of clamps. An example is the field Mushroom, *Agaricus campestris*. The cells of the mycelium that give rise to the fruit-bodies are multi-nucleate, as are those in the tissues of the sporophore. However, in the gill tissue as the hymenium is approached the number of nuclei in each cell decreases, and, as in other toadstools, the young basidium is bi-nucleate, the nuclei being of two compatible mating types. The mechanism by which this situation is achieved is not at all clear.

So far we have been considering only sexual reactions. It must, however, be remembered that most of the characters of the fungus are determined by genes carried in the nucleus. The segregation of these is an important aspect of basidiospore production. A fruit-body, although basically involved in spore production and liberation, is also a gene-shuffling mechanism.

Finally, it should be said that the mating system in agarics, particularly when both A and B genes are involved, ensures a high degree of out-breeding important for evolutionary flexibility. Perhaps this helps to explain the large number of species of toadstool that have evolved.

5 Nutrition and General Physiology

5.1 Requirements for growth

For the effective study of the nutrition and physiology of toadstools it is necessary to grow them in pure culture. A fungal culture on a medium solidified with agar is convenient to handle, but for precise nutritional work liquid cultures are necessary, since agar is by no means pure, but contains small amounts of a number of substances, especially inorganic ions. Most toadstools can be grown in culture, but by no means all can be induced to form sporophores even if care is taken to have the mycelium in the dikaryotic condition with the genetic potential to fruit. In consequence, detailed knowledge of the physiology of both vegetative and reproductive stages is limited to a small number. The toadstools most fully studied are the smaller species of *Coprinus*, and *Flammulina velutipes*.

The nutritional requirements for the vegetative stage of a toadstool are much the same as those for other fungi. Water is, of course, a necessity and is the major constituent of any medium satisfactory for growth. This must contain an organic source of carbon which is often provided as a sugar (glucose or sucrose) or as a more complex carbohydrate such as starch or cellulose. This carbon compound is, apart from the water, usually the largest single component of the medium. Then a source of nitrogen is necessary, either in an organic form such as an amino-acid, or in an inorganic state as a nitrate or an ammonium salt. Although all toadstools can use organic nitrogen, only certain species can assimilate it in the inorganic condition.

The other non-metallic elements that must be present in small but appreciable amounts in a medium that will support growth are sulphur, usually supplied in the form of sulphate, and phosphorus given as phosphate. Two metallic ions, potassium and magnesium, in quantities to be measured in milligrams per litre of nutrient medium, are also necessary. Unlike green plants, it appears that most fungi do not require calcium. However, as with organisms generally, a whole series of metallic ions are needed in trace amounts to be reckoned in micrograms, not milligrams, per litre. These include iron, zinc, copper, and possibly also manganese, molydenum and others. There is great difficulty in establishing the need for a particular trace element because of the problem of preparing a medium absolutely free from it and being sure that a sufficiency is not introduced with the inoculum. The significance of trace elements like iron, zinc and copper is that they enter into the molecules of certain essential enzymes.

All organisms have requirements for specific organic substances in minute amounts. These are vitamins and other growth factors, especially certain amino acids. A number of fungi, perhaps the majority, can synthesize the necessary range of these from simpler substances, so that it is not necessary to add them to the culture medium. However, quite a number of fungi are incapable of the full synthesis of the necessary thiamin (vitamin B_1) and there may also be an inability to make biotin and pyridoxin. Cultural studies indicate that a number of toadstools must have thiamin added to a defined medium if significant growth is to occur.

To give a more precise idea of the composition of an appropriate medium for growth and sporulation, one that has been used (MADELIN, 1956) for *Coprinus cinereus* has the following composition:

glucose	1.0 g
dl-α-alanine (an amino acid)	0.1 g
dipotassium phosphate	0.2 g
magnesium sulphate	0.02 g
thiamin hydrochloride	50 μg
water	100 g

This medium is slightly alkaline which is favourable for *C. cinereus*, although most fungi grow best on the acid side of neutrality (pH 7.0). It is, however, difficult to maintain pH at a steady level, for this may change as growth proceeds. A drift in pH may be due to unequal absorption of the cation and anion of a salt; to formation of acid (carbon dioxide or organic acids); or to the production of ammonia if the medium contains a rich supply of organic nitrogen.

This medium used for *C. cinereus* contains thiamin. This is not essential for the vegetative growth of that fungus, but no sporophores are formed unless the thiamin concentration in the medium exceeds 1 μg per 100 ml. Trace elements were not added to the medium but were, no doubt, there. Many workers ensure their presence by deliberate additions.

Certain of the components of the medium can be varied while still allowing growth and fruiting to occur. Thus certain sugars, such as fructose and maltose, can be substituted for glucose, but others (galactose and lactose) cannot be utilized. Also the insoluble carbohydrates – starch and cellulose – can take the place of glucose.

The actual concentration of carbohydrate is important. Glucose at 1% in the medium gives good vegetative growth and many sporophores, but if the concentration is raised to 3%, although vegetative growth is greater, fruiting is completely inhibited.

A number of nitrogen sources, such as peptone, can take the place of the alanine. Inorganic nitrogen, in the form of an ammonium salt, can be used and will allow fruiting to occur provided the medium is not permitted to become too acid following excess absorption of the ammonium ion. This can be prevented by adding calcium carbonate.

The needs of *C. cinereus* in pure culture have been considered rather fully. Those of other toadstools have also been studied and are found to be similar whilst varying in details. Such studies give much precise information about the nutritional requirements of a fungus. However, it is difficult from this kind of work to gain any clear picture of how a toadstool may behave in nature in a complex heterogeneous substratum and in competition with other organisms.

5.2   Temperature and growth

Temperature is a major factor in growth. In any fungus a minimum, an optimum and a maximum can be determined. These cardinal points vary with the particular species, but usually the minimum is in the range 2–3°C, the optimum 20–30°C and the maximum 35–40°C. The actual values may be slightly affected by the composition of the medium. The temperature-growth curve (Fig. 5–1) is asymmetrical around the

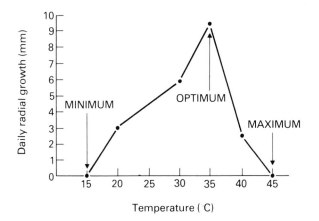

Fig. 5–1 *Coprinus cinereus*. Mean daily radial growth (over a four-day period) on nutrient agar at a range of temperatures. (Based on data kindly supplied by Professor J. Webster.)

optimum, the temperature interval between minimum and optimum being considerable, but that separating optimum and maximum being relatively small. In *C. cinereus* the cardinal points have relatively high values.

Temperature may operate differently on vegetative growth and on fruit-body production. Few cases, however, have been studied. Amongst the most interesting is the Honey Fungus (*Armillaria mellea*). Because of the great practical importance of this parasite (see p. 52), it has been studied considerably in culture, but investigators invariably found that it failed to produce sporophores under laboratory conditions. After many years the reason for this became apparent when it was discovered that for fruit-body production a temperature below 15°C is necessary, ten degrees short of the optimum for vegetative growth.

5.3   Sudden appearance of sporophores

The sudden appearance of mushrooms and toadstools has often caused astonishment. It has frequently been remarked that mushrooms spring up overnight. In fact the small primordium or button, usually more or less concealed, takes many days to develop, but its final expansion into a mature fruit-body that catches the eye is a rapid process. In this expansion few, if any, new cells are produced, the spectacular enlargement being the result of inflation of the individual cells. The situation in *C. cinereus* is illustrated in Fig. 5–2. Sporophore development is spread over about five days at 20°C, but spectacular growth is limited to

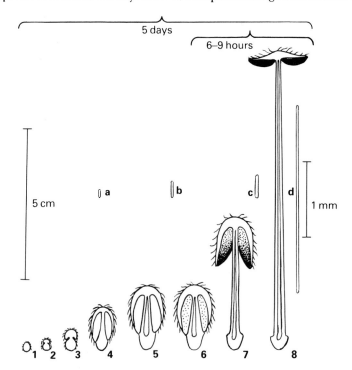

Fig. 5–2   *Coprinus cinereus*. Growth of sporophore from button stage (scale on left). Stages 1–5 completed in five days, but stages 6–8 cover only six to nine hours. A cell from the upper part of the stipe is shown in **a**, **b**, **c** and **d** associated with stages **4, 6, 7** and **8** (scale on right). (Diagram by Dr B. E. Plunkett based on data in BORRIS, H., (1934). *Planta*, **22**, 28–69.)

the final six to nine hours. During this period there is a considerable change in overall shape due to unequal swelling of cells in differing parts of the toadstool. In particular, the dramatic elongation of the stipe is due to the enormous stretching of its cells especially those just below the cap.

It might be expected that enlargement of the button into the mature toadstool would be due mainly to the intake of water. However, this is not so. In *Agaricus bisporus*, for example, the percentage dry weight in the fully grown mushroom is no lower than that in the button.

5.4   Influence of light

Light may be important for toadstools. In general it is without effect on vegetative growth, but in some species light is necessary for sporophore production. In *C. cinereus* no fruit-bodies are formed in total darkness, but the intensity of the necessary light can be extremely low and its duration short. The light that is effective is at the blue end of the spectrum (420–480 nm). However, not all agarics need light for sporophore formation. For example, it seems that the fruit-bodies of the Cultivated Mushroom can be produced in complete darkness.

Light may also have an important influence on sporophore orientation. Young fruit-bodies of most toadstools growing on wood or on herbivore dung are at first positively phototropic so that they grow towards the light. Later this reaction appears to die out and the stipe becomes negatively geotropic (Fig. 5–3).

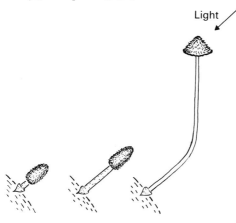

Fig. 5–3   *Coprinus cinereus.* Sporophore development in unilateral light.

5.5   Translocation

When an individual toadstool is developing, much material must be translocated through the vegetative mycelium to the region where the sporophore is forming. The mycelium is a highly branched system and, further, it is normally converted into a three-dimensional network by hyphal fusions (anastomoses) between nearby branches. A network of this kind would seem to be an ideal system for the translocation of material to a particular region.

Little is known about the mechanism of translocation, but the perforation of each cross-wall by a central pore no doubt facilitates the flow of material from cell to cell. It is worth noting that in toadstools there are no separate channels concerned with the flow of food and of water comparable with the sieve tubes and the xylem vessels of higher green plants.

One suggested mechanism of translocation involves the development of vacuoles in the cells behind the growing hyphal tip (Fig. 5–4). The formation of these drives the protoplasm forwards in the same way as the piston action of the vacuole of the basidium forces protoplasm into the enlarging basidiospores (see p. 18). Under the microscope the fine protoplasmic particles of a hypha can often be seen flowing from cell to cell through the pores, and apparently always towards the apex of the hypha.

As well as in the vegetative mycelium, material must also be translocated in the fruit-body. Movement of substances in the sporophore has been followed using dyes and radioactive tracers. There appear to be regular channels of translocation: ascent is usually in the inner tissues of the stipe and then there is a spreading out in the cap above the gills. In *Lentinus tigrinus*, a species that has been studied in detail, the inner hyphae of the stipe seem specially suited for translocation since

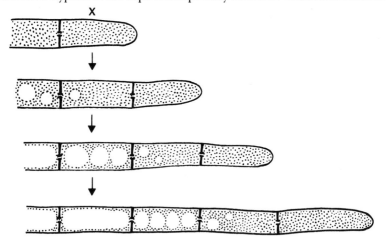

Fig. 5–4 Diagram of the tip of a monokaryotic hypha at successive stages of growth. The vertical series 'X' shows one cell as it ages. Vacuolation pushes the granular protoplasm towards the apex of the hypha.

they follow a vertical course, are practically unbranched, and have few cross-walls. The evidence suggests that translocation ceases when the sporophore is poisoned, for example with the vapour of propylene oxide. Translocation thus seems to be an active process and the sporophore is more than a wick.

5.6   Physiological activity of the hyphal tip

In the dynamics of growth the hyphal tip is of special significance, being the seat of great activity. It is making new protoplasm as well as receiving supplies by translocation from further back. In it, nuclear division is occurring involving the production of DNA. RNA is also being synthesized. Proteins, especially enzymes, are being assembled at the ribosomes; construction of phospho-lipids is under way, especially for the extending plasmalemma; precursors of wall material are passing out in the same region to build new hyphal wall; and hydrolysing enzymes are being extruded to dissolve insoluble food substances. To power these processes, the mitochondria are liberating energy in a controlled manner. In addition, substances are being absorbed, an activity known as transport, partly by passive diffusion through the plasmalemma but mainly by active absorption involving expenditure of energy by the hyphal tip.

5.7   Spore germination

The germination of toadstool spores often presents a problem for the experimental mycologist. Under certain conditions the spores of some species, such as *C. cinereus*, germinate freely. However, in a great many species basidiospores are hard to germinate, and in order to establish pure cultures mycologists usually resort to an inoculum from the inside tissues of a young sporophore. Work on the selection of improved strains of the Cultivated Mushroom was for long impeded by the extremely low levels of basidiospore germination achieved. Now, however, the factors involved in securing a reasonable percentage germination have been determined. Nevertheless, there are still a large number of toadstools, particularly in such genera as *Russula* and *Lactarius* where the conditions for any germination have not been realized in the laboratory.

6 Poisonous and Edible Toadstools and Mushroom Cultivation

6.1 Poisonous and hallucinogenic species

From ancient times man has been interested in toadstools. Certain kinds have been welcomed as food and some as inebriants, but others have been shunned and feared because of their known or suspected poisonous nature.

A few species are deadly, in particular the Death Cap (*Amanita phalloides*) and two closely related species. *A. verna* and *A. virosa*. These are responsible for most of the deaths from toadstool poisoning. Certain tests have been considered useful in distinguishing edible from poisonous kinds. It is said that if a toadstool peels, it is all right. But the Death Cap peels. It has been stated that if a silver spoon is turned black in the cooking, the species is poisonous. Again, the Death Cap does not have this effect on silver. Toadstools found in fields have been regarded as safe, but the Death Cap, though typically a woodland species, can occur in a field quite a distance from the nearest tree. None of the traditional tests has any validity. For anyone wanting to eat toadstools, the only safe way is to learn to recognize them on the basis of sound diagnostic characters set out in a reputable book with good coloured illustrations.

The medical picture of Death Cap poisoning is well established. For as much as a day after eating the toadstool the victim shows no untoward symptoms. Then the agonies commence with pains in the stomach, vomiting and diarrhoea. The patient may then seem to improve, but after a further day or two his condition again deteriorates and usually he dies. Post-mortem examination shows damage to both liver and kidneys.

The nature of the poisoning has presented considerable problems both in chemistry and in toxicology. In *Amanita phalloides* there are two poisons, both cyclopeptides: phalloidin, with seven amino acids in the ring, and amanitin with eight. It used to be thought that phalloidin was the villain of the piece. However, it seems that when this is fed to an experimental animal death does not ensue, but if it is injected into the blood-stream, the animal dies in a few hours. It would appear to be difficult for the phalloidin to get from the stomach into the blood, but once there it is a quick-acting poison contrasting with the rather slow action of the Death Cap itself. When amanitin is administered through the mouth, the animal dies, but only after a considerable lapse of time. Further, amanitin causes damage to both liver and kidneys, whereas phalloidin specifically affects the liver. The present evidence suggests that the pernicious poison in the toadstool is amanitin.

The Fly Agaric, *Amanita muscaria*, common in coniferous areas and birchwoods, is generally regarded as very poisonous, and its brilliant red cap with white spots seems to advertise this idea. However, it hardly deserves this evil reputation. It does contain a poison, muscarin, totally different chemically from phalloidin and amanitin and much less virulent. There is evidence that in the past Fly Agaric was eaten in Siberia to induce what was considered a desirable state of intoxication. Eating Fly Agaric apparently induced a kind of religious experience in primitive people and was believed to have divine properties. In the Vedic pantheon of gods, introduced into pre-Hindu India by peoples from the far north, there is a god of vegetable nature – Soma. A reasonable case has recently been made for identifying Soma with *Amanita muscaria*.

The Aztecs of Mexico employed certain agarics (*Psilocybe* spp.) in their religious rites. Indeed, in the remoter parts of southern Mexico these toadstools are still used in this connexion.

6.2   Edible toadstools

A considerable number of toadstools are edible, but no one should experiment with eating them unless he is fully familiar with the poisonous ones that must be avoided. In Britain, only a minute proportion of fruit-bodies for sale in shops and markets have been collected from the wild, and when these are on offer, they are almost always either Field Mushroom (*Agaricus campestris*) or Horse Mushroom (*A. arvensis*). However, in the markets of some Midland towns, stalls still sometimes display Blewits (*Tricholoma personatum*). The British and the Americans are, in general, highly suspicious of toadstools and few are prepared to eat any but commercially produced mushrooms. However, on the continent of Europe not only are certain of the larger fungi regularly collected for the pot, but they are also displayed for sale on the market stalls.

6.3   Mushroom cultivation

Only three toadstools have been extensively cultivated (Fig. 6–1). In Britain, the U.S.A. and Australia, production of the Cultivated Mushroom (*Agaricus bisporus*) is an important industry. Mushroom cultivation is an exercise in applied ecology and not a pure-culture process, except for the initial production of 'spawn'. Spawn, prepared in special laboratories, consists of dried pure-culture of the fungus impregnating sterilized compost.

On the mushroom farm, the first major operation is the preparation of the compost. Traditionally the starting point has been stable manure. This is horse-dung mixed with bedding straw and soaked with urine. With the shortage of stable manure many attempts have been made to find substitutes, but success has been limited. Compost is prepared in the

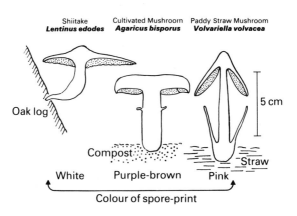

Shiitake   Cultivated Mushroom   Paddy Straw Mushroom
Lentinus edodes   *Agaricus bisporus*   *Volvariella volvacea*

Fig. 6–1   Characteristics of the three cultivated agarics.

open, stacked to a height of about a metre on a layer of hydrated lime. The compost heats and during the first week may reach 55–75°C in the middle. The heap is then turned over and this is repeated on subsequent occasions. By controlled watering, the moisture of the heap is kept at an optimum level. The whole process requires much skill and judgement. Thereafter the procedures are more standardized, are mostly indoors and pertain more to those of a factory than to those of a farm.

Mushrooms are usually grown in a special building on wooden trays (about 120 × 75 × 12 cm) stacked one above the other (Fig. 6–2). They are first filled with warm compost from outside and during the following week or so 'sweating out' occurs, the temperature first rising to around 60°C and then falling. When it is down to 25°C the compost is ready for 'spawning'. This consists of inserting pieces of spawn at a depth of 5 cm and 20 cm apart. For the next two or three weeks the mycelium grows in the compost with the temperature falling slowly to about 20°C, and during this period the moisture content must be carefully regulated.

The third week after spawning, when the mycelium has penetrated the whole volume of the compost, 'casing' with soil occurs. This is an essential process in the commercial production of mushrooms, although its physiological basis remains obscure. The casing consists of a uniform surface layer of soil, relatively free from organic matter, 1–3 cm deep.

Following casing, the trays are transferred to a cool 'crop room' where the temperature in the compost falls to 10–15°C. Again, care has to be taken to keep the trays at the proper moisture level. Several weeks now elapse before mushrooms are produced and actual cropping occurs. For some days a bed may give a good crop, followed by a marked decline, and then a week or so later productivity may again increase. This occurrence of 'flushes' is a special feature of mushroom beds.

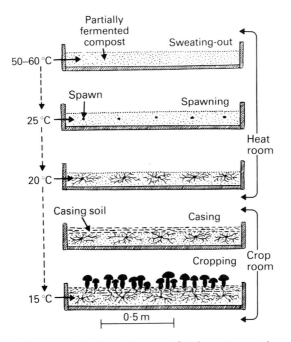

Fig. 6–2 Mushroom cultivation; diagram of indoor stages. The mushroom beds are in wooden trays.

During the whole period of growth and fruit-body production, various steps must be taken to control insects and fungal pathogens.

The Paddy Straw Mushroom, *Volvariella volvacea* (Fig. 6–1) is a pink-spored agaric with a universal veil which, when the stipe elongates, remains as a well-defined volva. It is grown in S.E. Asia on beds of damp rice straw. Cultivation, a side-line of other farming activities, is not nearly so sophisticated as is that of *Agaricus bisporus*. Pure-culture spawn is used only by the more progressive farmers, a portion of an exhausted bed normally providing the inoculum for a new one. The Paddy Straw Mushroom is either marketed fresh or, more usually, in a dried condition. It is a regular ingredient of Chinese dishes.

Shiitake (*Lentinus edodes*) (Fig. 6–1) has been cultivated for centuries especially in Japan. There the industry is as highly organized as is mushroom growing in Britain. The fungus is mostly grown on oak logs (5–15 cm thick and 1–1.5 m long) which are cut in early autumn when the sugar content of the wood is high. The spawn is normally obtained from a laboratory in which various strains of the fungus, suited to the different climatic regions of Japan, are maintained. It is supplied as a pure culture on small pieces of wood. These are introduced singly and snugly into holes drilled into the wood. Thereafter the fungus grows in the wood for several months and at this stage the logs are placed in a 'laying yard' where conditions are not too damp. If the logs are inoculated in the spring, the warmth of summer allows strong vegetative growth. After some six months in the laying yard, the logs are moved to the 'raising yard' where conditions are damper and the temperature is lower to encourage fruiting (Fig. 6–3). Logs remain productive for several years. Like the Paddy Straw Mushroom, Shiitake is usually marketed in the dry state.

The species described above are the only toadstools that are grown commercially on a considerable scale. All three have been in cultivation for centuries and there is an increasing demand for all of them. So far as *Agaricus bisporus* is concerned, around 50,000 tons were produced in Britain in 1978, compared with about 3000 tons in 1948.

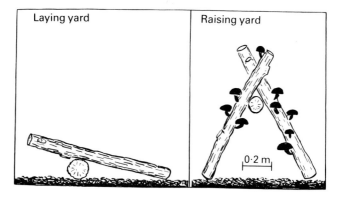

Fig. 6–3   Shiitake. Cultivation arrangements seen in vertical section. Left: oak logs in 'laying yard'. Right: logs in 'raising yard' bearing crop.

7 Habitat Relations of Toadstools

7.1 Difficulties in toadstool ecology

The ecology of toadstools is a large subject that is still in an unsatisfactory condition. What is most needed is quantitative knowledge of the part played by them in the whole ecosystem of woods and grassland. But the difficulties are great. It is hard to see how the biomass of the fungal mycelium could be estimated, because it consists of fine threads penetrating the substratum. With green plants the dry weight of the crop above ground can reasonably be considered as directly proportional to the total biomass. However, with toadstools the position is entirely different. It is a relatively simple matter to determine the dry weight of toadstool fruit-bodies formed in a given area in a year. Unfortunately this annual production from the perennial mycelium in the substratum varies enormously from year to year and cannot be related to the biomass of mycelium on which it depends. Further, it would be desirable not only to know this biomass, but also to have quantitative information about its activity. In this unsatisfactory situation all that is attempted here is to indicate some of the habitat relations of toadstools.

7.2 Seasonal occurrence

Toadstools are most abundant in late summer and early autumn especially in woods free from undergrowth. There they flourish until destroyed by the first severe frosts.

Just as each flowering plant has its season of blooming, so with toadstools species vary in the time of year when they fructify. A few are late spring species, for example St George's Mushroom (*Calocybe gambosa*) is found from mid-April to early June. In the main toadstool season, some tend to develop early such as the Tawny Grisette (*Amanita fulva*) which, if there has been enough rain, appears in late July, whilst others tend to come late like the Honey Fungus (*Armillaria mellea*) which is rarely abundant before September. *Flammulina velutipes* is common on dead elms throughout the winter even if this is severe.

BOND (1972) studied agarics from defined plots in the grass sward of an apple orchard in S.W. England over five years (Fig. 7–1). For each ten-day period he recorded the number of sporophores of individual species. About 20 were involved, the commonest, in decreasing order, being *Panaeolus foenisecii*, *Conocybe lactea*, *Conocybe tenera* and *Coprinus plicatilis*, all typical grassland species. The Field Mushroom (*Agaricus campestris*) was also frequent, coming sixth in the list, but, being relatively large, its

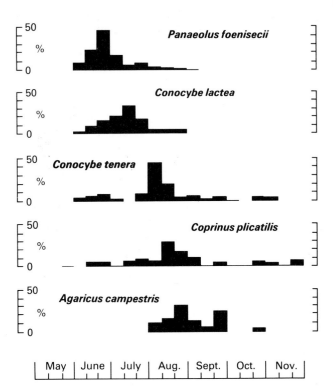

Fig. 7–1 Seasonal occurrence of toadstools in orchard sward. Histograms show percentage of total number of fruit-bodies of each species in each ten-day period, averaged over years 1964–68. (From BOND, T. E. T. (1972). *Trans. Brit. mycol. Soc.*, **58**, 403–16.)

biomass may well have exceeded that of species higher on the list. It is clear that different species tend to fruit at different times of the year.

7·3 Mycorrhizal and other woodland fungi

In a mixed area of woodland, with some beech and oak on the better soils passing over to stands of pine and birch in the poorer acid regions, a great variety of toadstool is to be found in autumn. Most are ground species. Some derive their food from the leaf litter; for example *Collybia dryophila* grows on oak litter, *Mycena sanguinolenta* on fallen pine needles, and *Laccaria laccata* on all kinds of leaf litter. However, many, particularly of the larger species, are mycorrhizal being in symbiotic relationship with the trees. Some are found only under certain kinds of tree. In *Boletus*, *B. granulatus*, *B. bovinus* and *B. luteus* grow under conifers, but *B. edulis* occurs under beech. *Russula* and *Lactarius* are noteworthy woodland genera, the latter being distinguished by the exudation of milky latex when the sporophore is broken. Species of these two genera tend to be associated with particular species of tree: *Russula fellea* with beech; *R. emetica* and *L. rufus* with pine; *L. turpis* with birch. However, *R. ochroleuca* is found under all kinds of tree.

An exacting procedure is necessary to demonstrate the mycorrhizal relationship between a toadstool and a tree. This involves joint pure culture of the fungus and the seedling tree. It has been used to determine which of the species normally found under pine are able to form mycorrhiza with its roots. The resulting list is a long one with species in the genera *Amanita, Boletus, Tricholoma, Russula* and *Lactarius*.

Most forest trees of temperate regions need to establish a symbiotic relationship with appropriate toadstools if they are to grow well on poor soils. These trees have fungus-roots (mycorrhizae) growing in the leaf litter. In a beechwood the mycorrhizae are easily seen if the deep layer of decaying leaves is disturbed. These particular rootlets are somewhat swollen, pale and closely branched, thus appearing coralloid. Around the root apex, including the region where root hairs would normally occur, the rootlets are enveloped in a closely-fitting mantle of fungal tissue. Cross-sections show that the hyphae also penetrate into the inter-cellular region of the cortex, but the individual cells of the root are not invaded.

Many centimetres normally separate the fungal mantle of the mycorrhizae and the toadstools of the forest floor, the two being connected by the fine hyphae of the mycelium. It would be impossible to trace this physical connexion; hence the necessity of pure culture procedures to prove the mycorrhizal relationship. This has been the subject of much elegant research. It seems that most mycorrhizal toadstools cannot use cellulose, the basic food for other forest species, but need a simpler source such as sugar. These simple carbohydrates are usually in short supply, any that may accrue to the soil being quickly utilized by vigorous saprophytic fungi and bacteria. However, in the roots of trees sugars are available and can be absorbed by the hyphae in close touch with the living root cells free from competition with other microoganisms. This might seem mere parasitism. However, it is now clear that the tree also gains from the presence of the fungus which apparently mediates a controlled supply of salts from the soil, being particularly useful in connexion with the absorption of the necessary phosphate.

7.4 Toadstools on wood

Dead trunks and limbs of trees support a large range of species. Some of these occur on only one sort of wood; others are more catholic in their taste. The Sulphur Tuft (*Hypholoma fasciculare*) is found on logs and stumps of both broad-leaved trees and conifers. However, some toadstools, like *Tricholomopsis rutilans* and *Paxillus atrotomentosus*, are to be found only on coniferous stumps. A number of toadstools are limited to beech such as *Oudemansiella mucida*, *Panus torulous*, *Pholiota adiposa* and *Lentinellus cochleatus*. Rather fewer species grow on oak, probably because of its high tannin content. However, *Mycena inclinata* is common in clusters on oak stumps.

7.5 Armillaria mellea, a parasite of trees

Most of the toadstools in a forest are playing a valuable role in breaking down complex organic matter, or in contributing more directly through the mycorrhizal association to the inorganic nutrition of trees. However, one abundant species is far from beneficial. This is the Honey Fungus, *Armillaria mellea* one of the most serious parasites of trees, although it is also capable of a saprophytic existence. Living trees cannot be directly infected by air-borne basidiospores. The fungus must have a saprophytic base from which an attack can be launched. Normally this is an old stump on which spores can settle and germinate to give a mycelium in the wood. Once well-established in the stump, *Armillaria* produces rhizomorphs composed of closely aggregated and more or less parallel hyphae. The rhizomorph, with a growing apex rather like that of a root, advances horizontally through the soil and may, in due course, make contact with the living root of a nearby tree (Fig. 7–2). Hyphae then penetrate and grow upwards in the cambial region to invade the lower part of the tree. The living tissue in the base of the tree is killed and in due course the tree

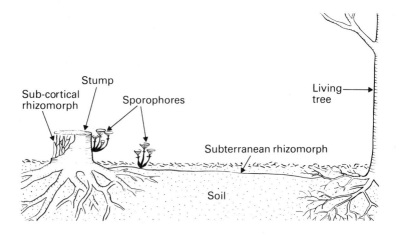

Fig. 7–2 *Armillaria mellea*. Diagram of mode of parasitism.

dies. The fungus continues to extend in the dead host growing upwards between wood and bark. In a tree killed by Honey Fungus, the bark readily separates and, if this is torn away, conspicuous sub-cortical rhizomorphs are to be seen forming an open network of black strands, like boot-laces, on the surface of the wood.

Attached to the base of a tree destroyed by this fungus, clumps of honey-coloured toadstools are to be seen in autumn. In addition, clumps often occur on the ground a little distance from the tree. If these are dug up carefully, their attachment to the black subterranean rhizomorph can be seen. The chief means of control of this ubiquitous parasite is to deny it any saprophytic base for attack by destroying stumps in a forest.

7.6   Grassland fungi and fairy rings

Grassland and lawns have their own fungus flora to which some reference has already been made in connexion with the sward of an orchard. An especially characteristic genus of grassland is *Hygrocybe* in which the sporophores have a waxy texture and are often brightly coloured. An especially striking toadstool of pastures is the Parasol Mushroom, *Lepiota procera*, with a cap often 20 cm across and with a relatively long stipe.

No account of grassland toadstools would be complete without consideration of the Fairy Ring Toadstool, *Marasmius oreades*. Fairy rings are complete or partial circles of dark green grass in a lawn or on a down. In summer or autumn a ring of toadstools makes a rather brief appearance associated with the ring. Many different species of toadstool are capable of giving rise to fairy rings, but the commonest is *Marasmius oreades*. A ring is not static but increases in diameter by 30–50 cm a year. Rings are known 200 metres across and these are estimated to be over 400 years old.

A fungal colony on agar starting from a central inculum is in the form of an enlarging disk. Its circular margin is occupied by hyphae growing radially outwards. Roughly the same thing happens in the soil. From its starting point the fungus spreads outwards at a radial rate of 15–25 cm a year, growing at the expense of the organic matter in the soil. After a number of years the colony may be several metres across and at this stage only the periphery is still alive, the centre having died. Certain regions are now recognizable in the fairy ring (Fig. 7–3). The most conspicuous is the circle of stimulated grass which is taller than the rest and of a darker green. This circle seems to correspond with the growing margin of the fungal colony in the soil below. A possible explanation of the stimulation of the grass is that the growing mycelium is liberating ammonia, in excess of its own need for nitrogen, during the breakdown of proteinaceous substances in the soil. The ammonium ion, or nitrate derived from it, would then be absorbed by the roots and lead to enhanced growth of the

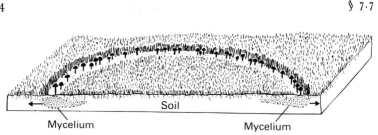

Fig. 7–3 Fairy ring. Three-dimensional diagram of half a ring on a lawn. The exposed front vertical section of soil shows the zone (stippled) occupied by the fungus advancing as indicated by arrows. Sporophores are formed in the bare zone. Outside, and in the centre, the grass is normal.

grass above. Just inside the dark green ring is one in which the grass is in poor shape, possibly because the fungus is seizing the lion's share of inorganic salts and water, and possibly also as a result of actual parasitic attack by the hyphae on the roots. Associated with this circle of dying grass, sporophores of the fungus make a rather brief appearance in late summer. In the central region of the disk, circumscribed by the ring, the grass is quite normal for the mycelium there has completely disappeared.

Some claim to be able to recognize a more complex structure with an inner ring of stimulated grass just inside that in which the grass is in bad condition. This inner ring is said to be due to autolysis of the ageing mycelium making available additional nutrients to the grass roots.

7·7 Coprophilous species

A number of the toadstools of pastures are associated with dung decayed to a greater or lesser extent. If freshly deposited horse droppings, a form of dung easy to handle, is kept under a transparent cover and given reasonable aeration, a rich fungal flora develops over a period of several weeks. During the first few days, mucoraceous moulds predominate, but in the second week small members of the Ascomycetes become dominant. Later, two to four weeks from the start, the dung bears a crop of small toadstools belonging especially to the genus *Coprinus* and including *C. cinereus*. Other genera are also represented, such as *Panaeolus* and *Stropharia*, but if species of these appear it is usually rather late in the succession.

All the coprophilous fungi that develop during the incubation of dung in the light seem to have the same dispersal story. The spores get on to the grass around the dung. In due course this grass may be eaten by a herbivore. The spores then not only pass uninjured through the alimentary tract, but may encounter there conditions that stimulate their subsequent germination in the deposited dung.

The late appearance of agarics in the coprophilous succession may be due to the fact that the time between spore germination and first fruiting is longer for them than for the other members of the dung mycoflora. The final dominance of toadstools may, however, be related to factors of competition. For example, it has been shown that hyphae of one coprophilous species, *Coprinus heptemerus*, can destroy mycelium of certain ascomycete competitors when contact between the two mycelia occurs.

7.8   Toadstools of special habitats

There are some rather special habitats for toadstools. Certain species occur on sand dunes, for example *Psilocybe ammophila* which seems to have a relationship with marram grass. Some grow habitually in clumps of

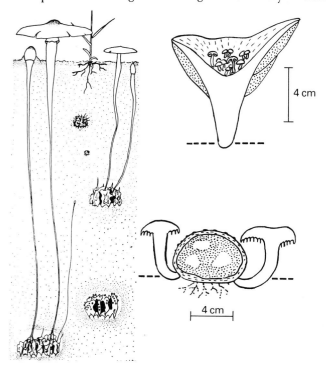

Fig. 7–4   Left: *Termitomyces* sp. Vertical section of lateritic soil forming part of an abandoned termitarium containing 'sponges', some producing pseudorhizae. On reaching the surface each pseudorhiza forms a sporophore. (Drawing by P. A. Dixon.) Top right: *Lactarius vellereus* (in longitudinal section) bearing tiny sporophores of *Nyctalis parasitica*. Bottom right: Earth Ball (*Scleroderma aurantium*) in vertical section bearing two sporophores (in vertical section) of *Boletus parasiticus*.

moss; thus *Sphagnum* cushions often support *Galerina paludosa* and *Omphalia sphagnicola*. Old sites of brushwood fires have their character-istic toadstools, such as *Myxomphalina maura* and *Pholiota highlandensis*, and some small agarics occur only on certain kinds of fallen leaf, for example *Marasmius buxi* on box leaves and *M. hudsonii* on those of holly.

There is an interesting relationship between termites and toadstools in tropical countries. The agarics concerned belong to a specialized genus, *Termitomyces*. In the heart of the termitarium are 'sponges' made of minute pellets of chewed leaves rich in lignified tissue. The termites use the sponge as food after it has been processed by the mycelium of *Termitomyces* which grows on the sponge in almost pure culture. The termites cannot digest lignified tissue, but can assimilate free cellulose and for the necessary conversion they rely on the fungus. The insects normally keep the fungus under control and it remains vegetative. However, it may gain the upper hand, and then fruit-bodies are produced. In sporophore formation a pseudorhiza (see p. 6) is produced that may be many centimetres long. This has a rigid apex which, as the pseudorhiza grows, pierces the cemented laterite of the termitarium. On emergence the toadstool itself develops, the end of the original pseudorhiza remaining as a hard 'umbo' in the centre of the expanded pileus (Fig. 7–4).

A few toadstools grow on the fruit-bodies of other larger fungi. Thus two species of *Nyctalis* are commonly to be found on certain of the larger kinds of *Russula* and *Lactarius*. Most members of the genus *Boletus* are mycorrhizal, but *B. parasiticus* lives a parasitic life on the Earth Ball (*Scleroderma aurantium*) (Fig. 7–4).

Further Reading and References

This list includes suggestions for further reading and also some specific references. Few references have, however, been given, except in relation to the mechanism of basidiospore discharge where so much remains unclear. The student is especially recommended to read Ramsbottom's book and, if possible, seek out the Buller volumes available in university libraries.

BOND, T. E. T. (1952). A further note on size and form in agarics. *Trans. Brit. mycol. Soc.* 35, 190–4.

BULLER, A. H. R. (1909, 1922, 1924, 1931). *Researches on Fungi*, Vols. I, II, III and IV. Longmans, Green & Co., London.

FINCHAM, J. R. S. and DAY, P. R. (1965). *Fungal Genetics*, 2nd ed. Blackwell, Oxford.

HARLEY, J. L. (1969). *The Biology of Mycorrhiza*, 2nd ed. Leonard Hill, London.

INGOLD, C. T. (1969). The ballistospore. *Friesia*, 9, 66–76.

INGOLD, C. T. (1971). *Fungal Spores: their Liberation and Dispersal.* Clarendon Press, Oxford.

LANGE, M. and HORA, F. B. (1963). *Guide to Mushrooms and Toadstools.* Collins, London.

LITTEN, W. (1975). The most poisonous mushrooms. *Scientific American*, 232, No. 3, 91–101.

MADELIN, M. F. (1956). Studies on the nutrition of *Coprinus lagopus* Fr. *Ann. Bot.*, 20, 307–30 and 467–80.

MULLER, D. (1954). Die Abschleuderung der Sporen von *Sporobolomyces* – Spiegelhefe – gefilmt. *Friesia*, 5, 65–74.

VAN NIEL, C. B., GARNER, G. E. and COHEN, A. L. (1972). On the mechanism of ballistospore discharge. *Arch. Mikrobiol.*, 84, 129–40.

OLIVE, L. S. and STOIANOVITCH, C. (1966). A simple new mycetozoan with ballistospores. *Amer. J. Bot.*, 53, 344–9.

RAMSBOTTOM, J. (1953). *Mushrooms and Toadstools.* Collins, London.

SINGER, R. (1961). *Mushrooms and Truffles.* Leonard Hill, London.